# Helter Skelter

# Helter Skelter

A Collection of Poems by Anita Philpott

Artwork by Grant Philpott

Matador
9 Priory Business Park,
Wistow Road, Kibworth Beauchamp,
Leicestershire. LE8 0RX
Tel: (+44) 116 279 2299
Email: books@troubador.co.uk
Web: www.troubador.co.uk/matador

ISBN 978 1784623 807

British Library Cataloguing in Publication Data.
A catalogue record for this book is available from the British Library.

Typeset in 10pt Palatino by Troubador Publishing Ltd, Leicester, UK
Printed by Ashford Colour Press, Gosport Hampshire

Matador is an imprint of Troubador Publishing Ltd

For Frankie, Lois and James

Take your dreams and run with them

A donation from the sale of this book will go to the following charities

World Vision UK – every child free from fear

Kidscape – preventing bullying, protecting children

# Contents

# I've found my Mojo

I've found my Mojo
Yes I've got it back!
Though nobody
knew it had gone!
Because, well!
Nobody thought it important
nor looked at me that long.

It may have been under
the sofa hiding on the floor,
next to the dog's bone near
the wellies by the door,
or in the wicker laundry basket
with all the socks and pants,
or in the spice cupboard
where sometimes we get ants.

But anyway, I've found it!

There was this *something*
I needed to do,
But I didn't think I would.
I went ahead and did it
And *d'you know what?*
It felt good!

I'm not saying *what* I did,
that's for *me* to know!
But you can see from
the smile on my face,
that I've found my Mojo!

# Skating

The wheels on my skates were metal
and they seemed to weigh a ton.
My friends had purring rubber ones,
mine sparked – like a gun.
We met outside our houses,
everyone went fast
round the green, along the street
and always I came last.
I wanted to get much better.
Mum said "There is a rink on the Pier,
maybe we'll go on Saturday,
as long as it's not too dear."

Here, people blurred past windows,
outside was a train on the track,
there were people laughing and skating
and skates lined up on a rack.
These skates had wooden wheels,
the rink had a wooden floor,
everyone went clockwise
under the clock by the door.
Now the best skater there
was this really old man.

He said he'd skated for England
and that his name was Stan.
He said that I was very good,
and I said that he was too.
He said I could learn to dance
and he'd show me what to do.
Every Saturday I would meet Stan,
he would teach me something new.
He taught me the waltz and foxtrot
and my confidence grew.
With the two-step and ten step
we were ready to compete
in our first skating contest,
Stan and my dancing feet.
In October that year,
the Pier burnt down,
I never saw Stan again
there or in the town.
So though I didn't become
a famous skating star,
someone once thought
that I really would go far.

# The Land of Old

Am I still in middle age
or is this The Land of Old?

I've got my teeth, got my hair,
now dyed a youthful gold.

If you ignore the love handles,
I'm a sight to behold,

with high heels on aching feet
and fluff on my Marigolds.

Each morning when I wake
there's the tiniest lapse in function,

there are minor niggles and aches,
that need some massage or unction.

Now is this the start of the final run?
And when will more inconveniences come?

I'm hanging on to middle age,
and hoping they make a pill,

to stop the coming of The Land of Old
for come it surely will.

# Booklover

Somehow you drew me in
there in my eyeline
understated in purple
with a subtle hint of gold.

Somehow you got my attention
the way you sat
not on your own
yet special and set apart.

Somehow the touch of your skin
your aroma warmed by my cheek
as I fell asleep
will remain in my memory.

Somehow what you told me
in those days changed me
lives with me
and makes me think.

# Storm

You can see it coming
Rain
Gathering darkly

The bird's chatter
Stops
Alerts stillness

Wind piercing leaves
Anticipates
A flautist's trill

As gusts cavort
Water
Spatters my face

Rain sheets sweep
Changing
Clear to grey mist

Sheltered in the doorway
Inhaling
Cloud fresh air

Corrugated rivers form
Gushing
A curtain before me

# Gorilla

People try to goad me
but bars keep them out.
They hurl things at me,
whistle, wave and shout.
Sometimes, someone,
an old soul like you,
stops and wonders
if I am someone, they once knew?
How I wish I could tell you,
dreams of another time,
of deep forest and hills
that I long to climb.
But I can't, no I can't,
little cousin of mine.
With so much compassion,
your guilt at being free,
your attempts to disguise both
your pain and empathy.
The language in your eyes
makes no worldly sound,
but speaks to my being
in this human playground.

# Laughter at the water cooler

I thought maybe I
wouldn't bother, but it was hot.
The water cooler beckoned. Too late,
he was there. Awkwardly he looked at me.
We smiled and then from somewhere deep within,
I felt a tickle welling up and a warming of the skin.
What was the trigger that made us want to snigger?
Why was it funny when we were hardly chummy?
A spitting loud explosion from a gaping silly grin,
a shaking off of burdens throwing caution to the wind.
Laughter exploded and stopped motion there and then,
disagreement imploded like some noisy sort of Zen.
Earlier troubles suspended, future plans now ended.
Now nothing can be dafter than a face full of laughter.
And nothing is as random as that sense of gay abandon,
the wonderful banality of spontaneous loud hilarity,
snorting made it worse and my mascara was a curse.
All thought processes were dead, worries left my head.
My body had been overtaken, I was physically shaken,
Now air burst from my lungs, it paralysed my tongue.
Convention collapsed, my breathing seemed to lapse.
Helpless laughter is freeing, joyous and just being.
This was a magic moment even with an opponent.
Exhausted by my chortling and snortling,
debilitated by my frivolity and jollity,

this whoopee cushion moment of life
ended as quickly as it had begun.
Brushing off the fun we reinstated our
chosen sensibilities and dispensed our water.

# Australia

on the way to school there was a puddle
the exact shape of Australia
in geography

I would always walk around it because
it seemed wrong to spoil the place where red
apples came from

anyway, I thought there was a hole and
I might fall through the Earth, all the way
to the other side.

when the sun came out the puddle would change
shape. I would jump into it splashing
mud everywhere.

the walk to school was boring all except
when it rained, then I would find my
Australia again.

# Ice cream Sunday

Yes that's right! You and Grandad watched Mum on the
helter skelter eating ice cream and she got it all over her.
*Oh yes dear, I remember that as clear as yesterday.*
*Good memories they were with your Grandad.*

Good morning Nan, did you have a good sleep?
How about going for a drive later, would you like that?
*Lovely dear, then can we go and see my*
*Mummy, she will wonder where I am?*

We'll see, but let me come round and see you first, it's
Sunday so we've got time. Chat about Grandad maybe?
*Who are you? why are you ringing me?*
*I am not supposed to talk to strangers.*

It's Bonnie your granddaughter, do you remember
I saw you yesterday Nan, we went to the park?
*I don't know you. You have never come to see me.*
*Is it time for my tea? Have we got cake?*

Look Nan see the amusements, looks like Butlins years ago!
Do you remember going there with Grandad and Mum?
*Oh yes we had such fun, Grandad took us on the big wheel*
*and all his money fell on the people below. Oh we laughed!*

Shall we get Rossi's ice cream Nan, vanilla out of the tub?
Just the way it's always been. Would you like that?
*Oh yes dear I would like that. Vanilla*
*was your Grandad's favourite, you know!*

So sit there on the wall now Nan, are you comfy?
That's good, look at the boats bobbing, can you see?
The tide is nearly in, look at all the children
covered in mud. I remember doing that!

It is so hot today Nan, be careful it's melting.
Here's a tissue. Are you enjoying that? Nan what
is wrong, are you crying? Do you want to go home?
*Mummy will be angry I have ice cream on my best dress.*

# Lucky

born on a blanket of stone
beneath an open window
on my own

in this cold wet world of birth
no-one notices me here
I am mute

then a shadow lifts me
plunges me beneath the steam
I breathe life

# The Last Haircut

Stroke – such a gentle word
such a cruel way to remove him
stroking him away, bit by bit.

He laughed after the fall
"Getting old dear,
need to watch the kerb."

The next time though, he went away,
a passing cloud held him gently,
then dropped him back, a little broken

I'm fine he says, as he sits precariously
on the kitchen stool,
trusting me.

As I stroke his head
the fragile strands of hair
float irrevocably to earth.

I do not let him see
the clump of his precious DNA,
that I keep in my hand.

# A new woman

*"Will I be pretty?" he asks of me*
I see the spectre of rejection waiting in the wings.
The bigots will hurt you distrusting such things.

*"Will my skin look like yours?" he asks of me*
Nature now tell, why did you form
those crumpled female wings unworn?

*"Will they like me?" he asks of me*
In a private agony to burst free,
to flutter, sun shafted, pubescently.

*"Will I look convincing?" he asks of me*
Pill plump, the kindest cut releases
unsure but joyful, the skirt uncreases.

*"Will I be happy?" she asks of me*
My world weeps. You are who you want to be,
but *I* was born a woman and you can never be me.

# The Pebble and the Shell

*This pebble will return to Earth*
*when man's day is done,*
*you are as good as any man*
*but better than none.*

*This has been to the Seven Seas,*
*to the Arctic and beyond*
*kissed by sea-nymphs in the deep*
*and sharks in the mighty pond.*

Beachcombing vagabonds we,
along the strandline of the land,
what adventures we might have
as we walk hand in hand.
While we hunt for more treasure,
seagulls squabble and soar,
in rock pools monsters lurk,
the Portuguese man-o-war.
Then amongst the bladder wrack,
I see a dazzling sight,
a whorled shell lay on its side,
iridescent perfect and white.

*When you put this to your ear,*
*you will remember today,*
*you and me upon the beach,*
*the waves and the ocean spray.*

Now, through tears
I hear the waves once more.
I hold the shell and am transported
to Cornwall's sandy shore.
My father has gone now,
he no longer walks with me.
I took the pebble to the beach
and threw it in the sea.

*You are as good as any man*
*but better than none.*
*This pebble returns to Earth*
*when man's day is done.*

# Tomatoes

I'm a banshee on my bike.
who cares if my knickers show?
Mum said I must be careful
on this dusty unmade road.

The sun is on my head.
Just a short ride from home
I see Mr Cranthorne's pigs,
by the jolly garden gnomes.

In through Mr Keyes' gate
whitened greenhouses stand.
I offer a crumpled brown bag
which he takes from my hand.

For that day we have company,
tea with my Uncle and Aunt.
Mr Keyes picks out the scarlet fruit
from orb-encrusted plants.

Delicious, warm and pungent
slurping, the pink juice flows.
I hope there'll be enough left
as I career down the road.

# Firewatch

6a.m and an early summer sun
hides behind the wall,
silhouetting the broken house

a yellow pinkness invades the waking
sky I feel uncomfortable, a voyeur
compelled to watch

floors are gone, lives are gone
only the fireplaces remain
bulldozed mortar and

yesterday's toppled bricks
dislodged memories of a
time fallen from favour

Mrs Green knits while her husband
is on lates and her shins turn puce
beside the fire

above her Jimmy stares into the flames
looking for a spark of inspiration
to help him finish his schoolwork

and on the top floor a young couple
give baby his feed and plan
for their glowing future

a shaft of red-gold catches the building,
briefly the fires are lighted again,
a living epitaph

by tonight the building and fireplaces
will be no more, the flame of the past
finally extinguished

# The Tree

Like a woman, unashamedly emerging from the bath,
sans hairstyle, make-up or clothes,
the tree in winter stands stark
vulnerable and glistening.

The voluptuous curves and contours of the trunk
lead on to unique wayward branches
as individual and welcoming as a woman's
outstretched arms.

Clothed in her luxuriant summer foliage,
the tree shows off her personality,
coquettishly she dances, swishing her skirt
to amuse the breeze.

Unknown colours catch your attention,
flash briefly, enticing you in, hinting at a
promise, a world of dark seduction
deep within her boughs

# Alcyone

Halcyon Days
when time
is mine.

When Earth says I am no longer of use,
I should like to be transformed by Zeus.
For then I can fly for ever more
spreading goodwill to distant shores.

Eternal Alcyone,
when I am she
I shall be

That beautiful bird that forever glides
skyward 'twixt moon and changing tides.
Cobalt blue plumes with green and red flash
I'll dive for my dinner with hardly a splash.

Kingfisher of ancient tale
welcome here.
All hail!

I am the honoured guest where 'ere I land,
but know like time, measured in sand,
that tomorrow I must fly once more,
spreading goodwill to those distant shores.

Halcyon Days
when time
is mine.

# The Cat

Where cirrus wisps shadow the viridian lawn,
she appears unannounced, sensual, warm,
voluptuous writhings in the July sun,
this is her Kingdom – she has come.
Rose tongue combing immaculate hair,
erotic ablutions with infinite care.
Floral sentries guard a Court of Green,
the Sun pays homage to this feline Queen.

# Sewing

A man came every week with a big box
of unstitched shirts that he put in the kitchen
for my Mum to sew.


She would sit with the treadle going up and down
all day long and I would sit on the floor
playing with bobbins.


This was called piecework, only I thought it was
about peace and I wondered
why it was so noisy.

# Birds' Eggs

With his all-weather skin
and grubby scabbed shins,
he collected birds' eggs
before it was a sin.
Down the lane by his home
wild land skirted the town,
before there were bulldozers
to take the trees down.

This land was my father's
where once he roamed,
Hunter, Fisher, Adventurer
through stream and loam.
He shared it with creatures
winged and webbed,
with slow worms and voles
and things you might dread.

The wind that rustled grasses
whistled, danced and ruffled hair.
He never forgot those days,
nor the music played out there.
Stalking in the brambles
something darts quick,
his boots are stuffed with paper
his new toy is a stick.

*Sprinkle my ashes,*
*where once I played*
*with friends from my childhood,*
*in this simple glade.*

Just one tree is still standing.
It has an undisturbed nest.
There beside the watching pond
his ashes now rest.
This Land of my Father
where once he roamed.
Hunter, Fisher, Adventurer
has now come home.

# Green Shutters

A pitchfork, time-wrapped in brambles,
gently taps on the door, no owner grumbles
at the strange knocking, no mistress flusters,
no dog barks, no child's noisy curiosity
inhabits this once conscious dwelling.
Only field life now makes this its home,
creepers growing unrestrained silence any pulse,
silvering leaves quiver, shimmering in unity,
gusts disturb serpentine fingers seeking hold.
They cling crawling into crumbling cracks
sealing night and day from sandy brickwork.

Two beetles duck and dive out of the wind,
jumbled leaves shimmy up the broken path.
The rusting arch of the old gateway sways -
dependent for its survival on the ashen, dark
fissured wood post, with pale lichen trace
-arthritic joints complain. Imperceptibly,
the grabbling unhurried plant entwines itself
trying to complete nature's festooned panoply.
One shutter creaking, still free, waves excitedly,
banging green against the frame in perpetuum
to jolt the sleeping house awake one more time.

# Facts of Life

We walked to the sandbank,
Jeannie, Ann and me.
Sometimes we would argue,
but today we agree.

The smell of oozy mud,
the sound of tinkling boats,
leaning landward, stranded,
in their own private moats.

We were thirteen, Jeannie and me,
her sister Ann was just ten.
In a book we had just found drawings,
about life and love and men.

Now at first we didn't believe it.
those people in the nude,
it looked so unlikely
uncomfortable and rude.

Although not interested,
we told Ann what we knew,
with diagrams drawn in the sand,
we doubted it was true.

The tide, was suddenly behind us,
in a gully called "The Ray".
We sploshed across the wet sand,
it was too dangerous to stay.

Now that was long ago
we are lucky we got away,
people still get caught-out
when the tide fills "The Ray."

Remarkably, what was spoken of,
turned out to be true,
what we thought of as *our* secret
every adolescent knew.

Though curious, we were innocent,
it was years before we planned
to put into practice,
what we had drawn in the sand.

## Sweet Dog

A scrummy funny
confection of a dog.
Marshmallow white
with three liquorice
smudges for a face.
Lay spread eagled
with neither fear
nor sense.

## Dawn Northern Spain

Night darkly fallen, oblivion is deep,
senses are uneven, as startled from sleep,
I see mounds and turrets, monsters with no name,
a vortex of fear in night's endgame.
Motionless now but will they attack?
Fearful to breathe, sweat prickles my back.
Suddenly a pale lustre starts to wash the east,
creatures become lighted, then each fearsome beast
slowly melts like snow, as man's oldest ally
lights them, row upon row.
Colour erupts silhouetting a tree,
a chink of hope makes fairy-time flee.
A song thrush sings her anthem
Rodrigo's string and plectrum,
hidden in the eluvia, still unlit by this spectrum.
The orb silently rises, this ancient ingénue,
a million times reborn to sparkle on the dew.
Reassured by newly green grass, I witness
the last spectre scurry and fade to grey,
the friendly orange that paints the hillside
rekindles my spirit, heralds a new day.

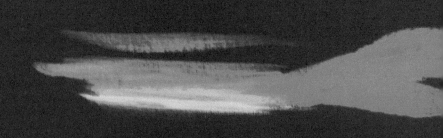

# Now I need to ask you

**Now did you hear? Last week on Monday when the Archers was on,
there was a noise, suddenly it went dark like the sun had *just gone*!**

I was in the bath, with candles all lit – a funny time I know!
At first there was a glooming shadow, followed by, a nameless glow.

There was an uncanny blast of chill air from somewhere unknown,
I had goose bumps multiplying and the candles now were blown.

Believe me I was too scared to move and I could not comprehend,
had Martians suddenly landed? Was the World about to end?

Then a whirring sound, followed by a repeated tick tick tick.
Dripping water, I grabbed a towel, I've never moved so quick.

I slipped, then went flailing, performing some airborne ballet,
I pirouetted, hit the door and the room faded away.

When I awoke it was sunny, The Archers tune was playing,
I shivered rubbed my head, felt the wet floor where I was laying.

Wrapped just in my gown I tentatively stepped on the lawn,
this strange unearthly incident seemed a fantasy, now gone.

There were boats in the estuary and seagulls on the beach,
I needed to talk to someone, if I could master my speech.

But one by one I phoned them to see what they had seen,
they thought it my wild imaginings and said, it had never been.

Someone then said there had been a thunderstorm way over Kent,
so the general consensus was that it was just, a non-event.

**BUT did *you* hear? Last week on Monday when the Archers was on,
there was a noise, suddenly it went dark, like the sun had – *just gone*...**

G PHILPOTT

# When the World was Black and White

A tiny flickering screen
was a mystery to explore
as in anticipation we sat,
cross-leggéd on the floor.

While cowgirls rode side-saddle,
Bill and Ben swayed,
The Third Man lurked in shadows
and Andy Pandy played.

Blue silhouetted figures,
in the light-extinguished room,
chiaroscuro faces
sat transfixed in the gloom.

Apologies then, for interludes
when, the potter's wheel spun,
clay was thrown again and again
but the pot was never done.

At the end of the evening
we would stand for the Queen,
turn-off and watch a white dot
disappear where she had been.

Ignorance or innocence
made our world seem right
back before I was grown
when the world was black and white.

Then the world changed to colour
with kaleidoscopic mobs
and expensive preening peacocks
and yellow spewing yobs.

Dishonourable wars
produced nothing but the dead
and natures drear disasters,
made the world turn red.

The screen became too small
for a spectrum that kept changing,
we demanded greater thrills
our expectations raging.

I wish that I could once again,
sit cross leggéd on the floor,
with the blanket of childhood
all black and white once more.

# Rooftop Jazz NYC

Mellow the music that touches the soul,
blue lamps reflecting in ice-clinking-bowls,
transfixed by a mood suspended within air
with solemn intent the musicians share
heartbeats, and soul beats from deep within
the bubble encased in a pulsing skin.

Music of passion dancing on keys,
and gold shafts on cymbals
and the patting of knees,
and drum-sticks that blur
turning riffs through time,
into mesmeric moments
of mood, scat and rhyme,
the spotlighted chrome
of black swivelled seats
lights a man in the audience
tapping his feet.

While the pianist-director flirts with chords,
there builds a great climax of this trio towards,
musical symbiosis, pushed into overdrive,
high-lighting the dissonance of our daily lives.

Blue lights and blue-notes
unite every seat.
Outside the bubble though
back on the street,
a real world exists
in the Manhattan below,
beyond skyscrapers that twinkle
where the red tail-lights glow.

## Snow

busy sound is silenced
by a spell of white
that shocks us with its stillness
stuns us with its quiet
mysterious statues where
once there were bins
footfalls are a blemish
that let the noise back in

# you are loved

when the perfect liaison is over
with promises tossed to the wind
when you are tired of being a rover
remember you are loved

when everything is going wrong
and your great plan did not work
when days seem dark and nights too long
remember you are loved

when the good news you long to share
needs a "well done!" a pat on the back
when money's scarce, when money's there
remember you are loved

when others judge your every move
small success never seems enough
when life's soreness needs a hand to soothe
remember you are loved

when you've got it wrong and feel alone
breathe in and let it go
when you know it's time to come back home
remember you are loved

when you reach the door that welcomes you in
no words are needed no answers sought
when I hold you close and touch your skin
remember you are loved

# Another Life

She leaves her outdoor face
on a hook by the door
next to her good coat
and her shoes on the floor.

She had danced with a Duke
and had friends galore
but now it is just her
and her shoes on the floor.

A Captain and Lieutenant
for her love had fought
she was mentioned in despatches
and talked about, at Court.

In clock-chiming-silence
she feels weak and sore
she wishes for conversation
people's shoes on the floor.

Once she made a promise
never to tell her tale
comely and courageous
this audacious young girl.

Her outdoor face was all
that they had known
"Did *you* really know her?"
"No – she was an *old dear* on her own".

Stamped official papers and secrets
tied-up in a drawer
were kept safely under her bed
with her best shoes on the floor.

## Suburban Lament

Realising a desire to leave
get out, unclench and breathe,
days serialised,
glintless deep eyes,
ideas maybe mildly arresting,
passed over, unworthy of testing.
Bland securities stifle all,
they crystallise, crumble, fall.
Intangible oppression surrounds,
tangible effects, now rebound,
suffocated by that cushion
that slowly ebbs away
with benign kindness
the substance of each day.

# Stolen

The sky at dawn is blue
the sun tops trees to the east,
I see grass renewed with dew
and I remember the robin's nest.

Crack! of a magpie's wings,
triggers my sixth sense,
a skirmish 'twixt fur and feather
till the cat flees over the fence.

Yesterday's perfect symmetry,
three heads with bulging eyes,
had queued jostling together
for their Mama's worm surprise.

Robins how hard you worked
foraging, day upon day,
we watched your devotion,
but we knew to keep at bay.

There are feathers on the lawn,
unimpressive, small and grey.
*Please tell me your babies fledged?*
*Tell me they got away?*

The empty nest is silent,
two robins skitter on the lawn,
now they must search together
for their babies, who have gone.

Birdsong has ceased
their loss hangs in the air,
this human heart aches
for a truth too cruel to bear.

# Lundy Bay

Sat on this knoll, laid thick with tough sea grass
I look at my companion, a Cornish snail
perfect in his lowly isolation,
a gentle gold and white personage.

Can it be fifteen years since I sat here,
looking down on centuries of rock falls,
a bead-box of shapes and tints washed
darker by the irrepressible tide?

For millennia the same sea has returned
crashing against this coastline uninterrupted,
this flamboyant master of waters
determines our very existence.

This great performance, this cacophony of parts
explodes, with such lavish showmanship, our
ringside seats are engulfed by nature's grandest
opera. The crescendo builds, touching every sense.

The colossus rises, arches its back, roars,
trembles briefly, then disperses into untold
droplets that rain down, like so much applause.
Gone. Soft sifting wet notes tinkle melodically

until the next great event bursts upon
the rocks. A lone seagull finishes his
duty as sentry and swoops hard at me,
protecting his patch, screeching overhead.

Nothing here changes. Nothing ever will.
Sea compose your music, until I return.
Goodbye dear snail, may you survive
till I find my way to this knoll, sometime soon.

# Blue sky dreaming

It was a day for blue sky dreaming,
youthful imaginings, vague schemings,
warm sunned bodies with a single aim,
friendship and the promise to meet again.

Blowing dreams into balloons, we let fly,
arousing passion in a rainbow sky,
dot after dot we watched them disappear,
There Be No Dragons and we knew no fear.

1913, the last summer we would run wild,
adolescence was approaching, we were beguiled.
Our world was changing, I was no longer a child.
On that blue sky day for us, the Earth smiled.

# The Edge of Everything

Here on the Edge of Everything
where sky plunges into sea
where land and sea swap identity briefly,
until the sea takes back control
I walk in harmony with the subliminal music
of waves and slipping sand and seabirds and grass tempered wind,
and always my heart keeps time.
I listen to the contrasts of shape and colour,
the music of the moment, and my feet must keep time.
What is spiritual? What magical?
This land of ancientness with its traces of other existences,
feeds a new curiosity, that becomes a crucible for my imagination.
A dangerous place – but full of what can be.
Keep time, be still and listen -
this place will feed your being.
Feast on it while you may.

Marathon Mantra

bumping, clumping
starter gun goes,
pumping heart beats
up on my toes,
break from the clump
now, out of the row,
must get a move on
training now shows,
settle the pace down
puff breath blow,
there is a gap now
as the group slows,
clumping, thumping
gasping air flows,
thumping, pumping
blow follows blow,
heart pump leg crump
make the blood flow,
halfway hard way
make the legs go,

uphill steeper
blow follows blow,
chaffing, soreness
going too slow,
check time, keep pace
up with the flow,
downhill-mile, good,
blisters on toe,
wall now pain-how!
blowing, gasp, blow.
twenty mile slump ow!
legs become dough,
too many pass me
does my face show?
pulse now thumping
blow follows blow,
salt sweat stinging
just a stone's throw,
crowd noise jumping
FINISH banner grows,
heart keep thumping
now GO LEGS GO!

# For Life

When first you touched the skin,
were overwhelmed by the smell

of living and saw the fontanelles
pulsating with hope, you knew that

this was for life. You watched over
hourly, checked for every breath,

new word, cleaned every smudge,
smell and indiscretion as if it were

your own. This umbilical parasite,
this ungrateful extension, saps your

love, life and ambition. But if he
needed more you would make a pact

with the Devil to ensure his survival,
to keep him safe. This is your child.

# Hadleigh Castle

Proud grey walls rest on a hilltop steep
both mundane duty and noble feat
saw brave souls toiling raw man-brawn
determined steps, made this manor born.
As seasons travelled their fertile way
from cold sea mists through the haze of day
sweat-reeking ditcher wrought his moat
dust choking mason his stonework smote.
While towers repelled the old Gallic threat
within warring walls their weapons whet
Lord Hubert surveyed his dream fulfilled.
His castle honoured those ancient guilds.

Proud grey walls rest on a hilltop steep
as relaxing families recline replete
ice cream moments melt – to run, to fly
to roll down-hill with blithesome cry!
Youthful exuberance scales rag-stone walls
real story-time towers makes warriors all,
dark dungeons abandoned are now gone,
freedoms, new constraints, life journeys on.
Drawn by shadows to these ancestral grounds
echoing passions of past peasant sounds,
modern man surveys these lands at will.
His castle honours those ancients still.

# Giant

with slippered toes on Giant's feet
we'd laugh or sing a song
safe and never wavering
through life we strode along

if my footfalls were unsure
he would always provide
a way to climb aboard
those feet to ease the ride

my steps though grew steady
and I could walk beside
equalling his purpose
equalling his stride

then he started to falter
shaky in his stride
I had to decline
his offers of a ride

his slippered feet now unsure
are happy to trust mine
the sun throws down a shadow
of the Giant's outline

# Under the pier

Drawn in by the wide yawn of barnacled girders
my skin buzzes with vibrations from overhead trains,
as the shingle beneath my feet begins to move
a gust suddenly turns my hair into a wind vane.

Iron tracery, clean, black against the bright sky,
while close-by gulls land, picking at discarded chips.
Their squabble echoes as they fly towards the sea.
A pattern of worm casts, small salty walnut whips

with random bubbles from deep below, ragworms
safe from bait-diggers' spades, doing what they know.
The sea will wash over, feeding this other world,
their history meets ours, it has always been so.

The glinting stripe of the incoming tide has widened,
welling up ever deeper in the estuary.
Soon with great certainty it will come, wash beneath
this pier, claim back, flush me, from my sanctuary.

Beautiful black cradle, each generation anew,
discovers these arms. Though there is no forever,
let loving and laughter ring from under your shadow,
may you still stand, as testament to man's endeavour.

# Butterfly Summer

Fluttering skirts
with inaudible sound,
flight patterns human eyes confound.
An incredible collection of
impeccable perfection,
as the butterflies
return.

# Moontide

The Moon's reflection, a fractured twin
astride the pulsing tide. Benign steward
whose gentle glow threatens a dark privacy.
Sandy mud oozes through my toes,
soft lapping water creeps ever closer,
gulping ozone smells, shell-flesh tastes,
the brown green happiness that once
stained our legs and dried grey and
flaky, reminds me of distant laughter.
Soon it will be time.

Out there, fathoms deep, wet-life
swimming, spawning, salt and mud
bedding in new life, simple hopes.
Human life too, the sea shanties
of dead men buried cradling bombs.
Mislaid dreams, dance across the
water to serenade the night
putting my oneness in its place.
A seal cries on a distant sandbank.
Soon it will be time.

Fishing boats suctioned into stillness
wait for the soft lapping to return, ropes
jiggle harmonising with the wind, tinkling
frivolous music masking a humble life,
the beauty of toil measured not in riches.
Thrashing marsh grasses, dredged crusty
with sand, whip my legs to wake my senses.
Water floods the sandcastle, the moat gone.
Did they think it could last forever?
Soon it will be time.

Creation of crenulations and tunnels
made glorious by imagination. Innocence
washed away into so much bitter chyme.
Under the veil of darkness sleeping children
plan tomorrow's sweet adventure. Restless silt
shifts throwing me off guard. Am I truly ready?
Now ankle-deep, wet-life swims around me, the
soft lapping has returned. Sparkling ripples
expose me in the moonlight. The boats bob anew.
It is time.

## Plastic World

with plastic smile
covering a plastic mind
she proffered my plastic burger
a plastic coffee
in a plastic cup
I with plastic soles
take plastic steps
over shiny plastic tiles
to my shinier plastic seat
and there survey
the shine-less
plastic world outside

# Beneath the sign for Craven A

He will wait.

where he always waited – beneath the sign for *Craven A*.
Here he licks the hop wet floor,
drinkers are reflected in bright optics
not seeing the yellow dog by the door.
Swathes of smoke rise above beer fumes,
laughter bubbles pop
then come to rest in a lonely corner.

He will wait.

In a booth, holding hands a tryst is made,
across the table sexual chemistry begins to brew.
The dog feeds on crushed crisps beneath the chair
as their feet touch. No scent of his Master, no clue.
Love found and lost. He senses the voice that
wrapped itself around him for so long, but has gone.

He will wait

The oil rag – brilliantine – tobacco still lingers,
the old odour he knows so well,
who is the stranger who sits in The Chair?
Could he help? Is he a friend? He cannot tell.
A pale imitation of his Master, though
like the leaves on the trees
soon he too will flutter away.

He will wait.

Too soon the Bell clangs, "Time gentlemen please!"
Still time. Yes! Maybe tonight he will be here?

But coats move on people who ruffle his head.
He hears "nice dog." The day's-end draws near,
as pat follows pat a disappointing silence fills the room.
The Chair is now empty. Everyone has gone.
Hope extinguishes with the lights. "Night fella."

The loping figure passes into the shadows of Dark Lane.
He will be back and sit beneath the sign for *Craven A*

to wait yet again.

# Sweet Peas

A posy of sweet-peas tied with string. "These are as pretty as you."
I smiled, accepted, it was honestly meant, he loved me, one of the few.

Always for me, the first tender bunch, mauve and flesh pink.
Swirling tobacco curls around the memory. I think

I know, when summer has arrived, because they appear,
the same time, give or take, about now, every year.

As significant, as ephemeral as a first kiss.
As delicate, as vulnerable as a butterfly wing.

As aromatic, as wondrous as a baby's soft breath.
As enchanting, as the porch on a barmy summer's night.

Now I see them in the florist's bucket. Transfixed,
for that moment, I believe that I am pretty.

Their scent engulfs me and there he stands, once again
with his proud calloused hands and warm tobacco grin.

# The tree that was bowed

We trod the way from the stile by the road,
down overgrown paths by the tree that was bowed.
A little grey rabbit blocked our way,
"Hello Floppity, have you had a good day?"

He and the sun disappeared o'er the hill.
We then laughed out loud and time stood still.
I see a grey rabbit now, surely not the same,
there is no light and it begins to rain.

I get to the cove where waves crash below.
It is dark and cold, my progress is slow.
I'd fallen, not badly, he'd gathered me in.
Hidden passions surfaced as skin touched skin.

Sea heather and ferns had lined our route,
as the moon rose, we heard an owl hoot.
Now, the slippery shale throws me to the floor,
in just the same place that I'd fallen before.

We'd lain on our backs, chose our own special star,
to remember the moment, that we'd come so far.
And now with the sun, fallen to it's rest,
struggling with emotions constricting my chest,

I climb up the headland above the sea
where once white horses had pranced for me.
Now I search for that star, his and mine
that had seemed so important at the time.

But without him here it matters nought,
it is he and that moment that I sought.
This is the last time I will return,
with salty tears I believe I've learned

to accept my life, with no going back.
I will not linger and set off on the track.
I retrace my steps to the stile by the road,
down overgrown paths, by the tree that is bowed.

# Earlier

Earlier there had been family, a BBQ celebration and my coming of age,
as crickets in unison herald the dawn of our night, we young men
embarked with joy towards endless possibilities and potent dreams.

Languorously displayed in the half-light he lolls absently,
a romantic statue that draws us in, our front man and we
his groupies who hang on every word.
Later, laying in dry corn behind the house, smoking,
light-years away from the sleeping household we talk
of music and fame and improbable futures.

Later, years later, when life's grinding purpose is realised
we might hear Him mentioned, this rock-star God.
He has lived the dream, our dream.

Later still, we heard that He fell, we knew not why or how.
Then He rose again, so a new generation of festival disciples
could follow, entranced by the enigma.
Compelling attention, he took them to a place only he knew existed,
fed their souls with what could be. Like us, they might only guess
at the demons of his dark hours.

Earlier there had been family. Celebrity and his life had now
come of age, we stood smoking, grown men, reminiscing about
music and fame and old dreams and the vision he had given us.

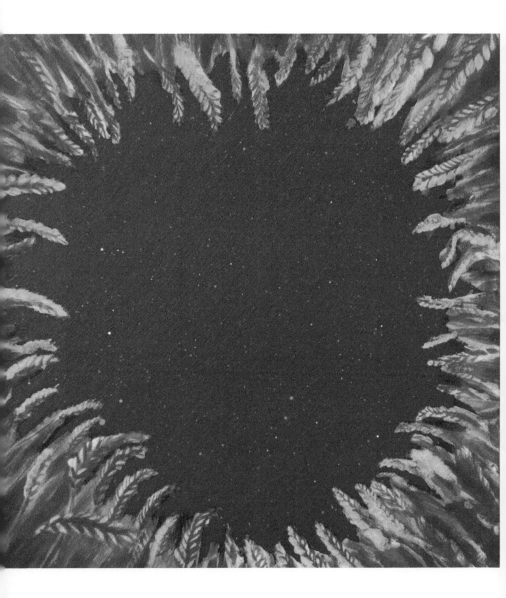

# Bluebell Wood

My journey is long
on this warm May Day,
lapwings by a stream
put on a display.

A gentle sloping path
leads down to some trees.
I muse at the prospect
of resting 'neath these.

I enter a canopy,
dark and green,
and through ancient
coppicing, in between.

I see a jewel-like hue.
so intense,
so vibrant
and so blue.

Perfect, luminous,
lazuli bright,
like a moth I am drawn
to this wondrous sight.

Through blind alleys
and thickets, high as my chest,
stumbling, I push on,
with the promise of rest.

I see a mound of grass,
so dense, soft and deep.
at peace now I stand,
with happy, bare feet.

With sculptured bark,
imprinting my back
I see ants carry baggage,
up the dusty, grey track.

"Sky you are not welcome here"
lichen and toadstool tease,
as leaves on branches,
flutter, high in the breeze.

See now, playful Puck
flits from bower to bower,
shooting lighted arrows
to the heart of each flower.

All knowing ancestor,
what sights have you seen?
here, did weary horsemen,
swear allegiance to their Queen?

Did deer, and bears
once roam these parts.
and clandestine lovers
risk death after dark?

This carpet is too perfect,
for my imperfect tread
and makes me contemplate
what lies ahead?

For life is so fleeting,
can be snuffed out with a puff
here I am, at-one with Nature
and for now, that is enough.

# Rain

we spin around on the grass
human windmills whooping aloud
a sprinkle of rain turns to hailstones
as we dance under the cloud

spinning around arms thrown out
faces upturned to the rain
water trickles down our backs
as we spin again and again

my cotton dress is soaked
and stuck pink to my skin
and the worms' heads start to
emerge wondering at the din

# My beach

That holiday I went to bed watching through the round window.
I longed to be down *there*. When I saw dawn's morning glow
I was up! I saw the water coming in and leaving "Tide's Reach"
with my towel under my arm I raced alone to the beach.

Nobody else saw my magic, this was mine, my own domain.
The sea and the waves were all for me, my very own game.
The sands were a pale desert of ripples and a flatter
than flat expanse just waiting for my footprints. I pattered

over slippery seaweed into the surf, skipping and jumping
screaming unheard. A huge curling wave hit me hard, thump
it pushed me under the foam, I disappeared a wet salty dipping.
Desperate for air till I bobbed above the thrashing blue, dripping

with joy and resolve. I stood my ground once again wanting more,
huge rollers that sprayed like geysers as they hit the rocky shore
scared me but made me feel alive, braver than at any time.
Through the round window, I was invincible, the beach was mine.

# Throb

Nature is deaf and blind to men's quarrels
with poise she seeds, balances and grows,
ignoring all our human disasters,
inventing beginnings on pointed toes.

The freezing challenge of ice, the charring
of heat means she must reinvent her stance,
diversify, change position, if she must.
Stunned briefly by man's sterile dance

she always survives with novel choices.
She tried once to speak but no one listened,
she has forgotten how to argue or to try
but her work goes on and on and on and on.

Hemlock, the devils purse, and sweet grasses,
poisonous, benign, beneficent are hers. Waters
surge and flow and gush then disappear, no
matter what man thinks he has invented

to change it. She covers over the blood that
is spilled and the bodies that have fallen, the
good and brave beside the stink and hopes of
small-mindedness and greed. Scrambling over

fortresses and barbed fences festooned with
human flesh, slowly and continuously, when
their backs are turned, she grows, reclaiming
what is hers. Trees are her sentinels around

which transient man musters for battle.
This visionary is supreme, no voice
to rise in anger, no dispute to be had.
Choking and dying and the bitter remorse,

the confessions and the honour and the
point-of-it-all, of course! Everything,
yes everything, eventually subsumed.
These sorry tenants cannot win. She owns

this land, not inconstant men; there are simple
poppies and ivy that creeps and brambles
that seep into any free space while Nature keeps
dancing to the throb of her own heartbeat.

Beat beat beat beat beat...

# Best friends

we best-friends-forever lived next door
we shared the same outside space where
we skipped bumps and pushed dollies
round the green in our matching prams

we shared the same boyfriend which he
really seemed to like and we shared our
pink bubble gum too hiding from our
parents behind next door's rickety shed

we shared the climb up the big elm tree
did handstands on the grass verge and
shuffled about on our sisters' stilettos
bloodied thumbs to seal our life's bond

we shared a bed sleeping head-to-toe
we joined Brownies collected badges
convinced our Mums to buy our first bras
and on the way to school we shared dreams

we best-friends-forever would never forget
but we would one day seek greater thrills
as we stepped gingerly into a world of
sharing with new friends beyond the road

# Helter Skelter

# Perfect picture

At 17 I had this picture in my head of my perfect man.
He was six foot and handsome and he would love me.

When I met you it all seemed to have come true, we
fell into each other, with laughter and ideas and love.

You were that picture, I felt charmed, frightened in case I
broke the spell, the sight of you made my tummy turn over

and my brain come alive. I came to know every line, dip
and angle of your face. I loved the way your eyelashes curled,

the fine down on the top of your ears, your dimples. Above
all I loved how we were better together. You were funny and

I liked the way people were drawn to you, how you made me
smile at old jokes, how modest and honest you were.

I sketched you endlessly, making that vision I had imagined
real and fearful that the warm glow I felt, might disappear.

I was always the crazy one with mad notions but you were
happy to be a little reckless sometimes, we had fun planning.

You were kind and generous. You wanted me close to you
but let me run free. I was proud to have you by my side,

my perfect picture. I understood why your mother always
adored you and I was happy to share that adoration with her.

I didn't know then, that this would be our forever but it has been.
Thank you for making a 17 year-old girl's dream come true.

# Notes on Poems

*Gorilla*
During the 1970s a gorilla became the face of London Zoo, he was called Guy. It was a time of change, when the morality of caging animals was highlighted. In this poem I tried to put myself in Guy's place.

*The last haircut*
This poem was written about my father, I still have a lock of his hair. The poem was entered in the 2014 Poetic Republic Poetry competition. It was selected for the anthology and is included in the e-book "Poems to Talk About 2014."

*Alcyone (al-sahy-uh-nee)*
Alcyone is the name of a character in Greek mythology who was changed into a kingfisher. When she flew, which was for a few days each year, it is said the Gods stopped all storms and created a state of calm. It is from Alcyone that we have derived the term *halcyon days* meaning a short period of calm.

*A new woman*
In my other life, I work with trans-gender clients during transition from male to female. I try to give emotional support but sometimes feel I cannot be as honest as I should be because I want to help build self-confidence and not crush hopes for the future. This "new woman" is an amalgam of many such people that I have met over the years.

*Another Life*
In 2010 it was reported in the national newspapers that the body of an elderly woman had been found. Under her bed, were discovered, classified documents and war honours from WW2. Nobody knew who she was or where she had come from. This inspired me to write a poem. A year or so after I wrote this imagined story, her life events were revealed.

Her name was Eileen Nearne, code name Rose and in WW2 she was a member of the SOE, the Special Operations Executive. She was sent to France as a radio operator as she spoke fluent French. She was arrested, tortured and sent to Ravensbruck concentration camp. She eventually escaped; she was decorated for her bravery by both Great Britain and France. After the war she settled in England but chose not to talk about her wartime experiences.

*The Edge of Everything*
This poem was written after visiting Holme-next-the-Sea in North Norfolk, England. This is a place of wide-open spaces and wind. The sea's power is unchallenged. At low tide a wooden *henge,* approximately 4000 years old can be seen, almost buried beneath the sand. Due North of this coast lies several thousand miles of open sea before the next landfall. Here there is a sense of isolation made greater by the evidence of ancient man.

*Beneath the sign for Craven A*
I wrote this after the smoking ban came into force in the UK. I was in an old pub with wooden benches in Yorkshire, England and noticed an enamel sign advertising cigarettes. It said *Craven A* and written under this was the strap line *"will not affect your throat"*. It was put up there a long time ago. I thought how times had changed and imaged the pub full of people, tobacco smoke and a devoted dog waiting for his owner.

# Artwork & Images Index

Artwork by Grant Philpott

*Acrylic on canvas*

*Oil on canvas*

*Pen & Ink Watercolour*

*Lino prints*

Photos by Anita Philpott copyright 2015

# Biographies

## Anita Philpott

Strange events, a snatch of conversation, the wonders of nature, love and loss or just a funny idea, prompt me to write poetry. This collection is a celebration of some of these. Poetry can take you anywhere you want to go and be whatever you want it to be. I believe poetry is best spoken aloud and I am happy to read to anyone who would like to listen. I am lucky to be surrounded by a family whose creativity and joie de vivre makes life interesting and sometimes unpredictable. I live close to the estuary of the River Thames, a constantly changing backdrop and a positive influence on my writing and thoughts.
Anita runs a busy clinic and is married with 4 sons.

## Grant Philpott

Grant has created artwork & illustrations for print, television, theatre, exhibition and the national press. Grant is a TV Producer & Director and lives in Leigh-on-Sea, Essex.

# Acknowledgements

Thank you to everyone involved in the production of this book.

To my son, Grant Philpott for his delightful artwork, without which this would be a very different publication, for the long hours he spent knocking the book into shape and for just being part of the process. It has been fun.

To John who listened the most.

To Ryan, Sebastian and Barnaby for listening to my ideas when their heads are already full of their own.

To Frankie, Lois and James, my grandchildren and for the joy they bring.

To Mel for humouring me.

To my parents for creating such a curious individual.

To Christine for her love and enduring friendship and for helping to edit the poetry.

To Lisa for always listening and for being so encouraging.

To Chris Edwards who suggested the book.

To all my friends and clients who keep me sane and happy!

To everyone at Troubador for their advice and support during the publishing process.

And finally to all those poets who have entertained and inspired me.